How t

to Anyone

10 Secret Tips You Wish You Knew

Jonathan S. Lawson

CONTENTS

Introduction

I want to thank you for purchasing this book. Since you bought it, you probably have problems talking to people, and that is okay. First off, know that you are not alone. This problem affects millions across the globe every day. Secondly, congratulations on making the decision to making a change. It takes a strong person to recognize that there is a problem, and an even stronger person to do something about it.

In this book, you will find information on possible causes of this problem, and information comparing today's age to the older days, to see if there has been a change in the overall communication over the years, to figure out if that alone could be a problem. You will find ten secrets to help you be a better communicator, and help you get over any problems with communication you may have.

By the end of this book, you should be able to talk to even the most distant of strangers. You will have some things to practice, that will make you a better conversationalist, and you will even be able to initiate a conversation without any awkwardness. Enjoy!

Chapter 1

Before We Begin

Before we jump right into the secret steps, there is some basic information that you should know. This will help you to better understand the basis of your communication block. In truth this world is a lot different than it used to be back in the days of covered wagons and community bathing, but maybe, it isn't better in some ways. Yes, now we have technology and indoor plumbing, but there is a haze over us that maybe is not as friendly as it used to be.

People call this the age of communication, based on the ease in which we can talk to people miles away from us. That is a great thing in all, but how about the people that are right next to us? Over seventy percent of the world's population admits to having a problem with communicating properly with people in their own families, and they definitely can't hold a proper conversation with strangers or basic acquaintances. This is a problem, but is it really so different than the days of yore? Let us compare, shall we?

In the old days (before telephones were in every household, even before the invention of the telephone) it was so much easier to talk to people face to face. That is because for the longest time, it was the only form of communication, other than the post that came every week, or the occasional messenger pigeon that often took days to reach a destination seventy miles away. If you wanted to have a full on conversation in real time with someone, you had to go to their house, and talk to them. This meant that communication was futile to survival, because if you needed something you had to ask for it. You would have to communicate regularly with everyone around you. Walking down the street, it was customary to greet everyone with a smile, and a "hello, how are you today?" To not do so was considered bad manners.

Humans had to interact by speaking several times a day, and as a result, everyone was more friendly to each other, because you never know when you might need their help. People regularly dropped by their friends' houses unannounced and unplanned, because they had no way to call ahead to see if they were available. These visitors were not turned away, they were greeted with open arms. Children came in to greet the guests, before being sent back outside to play, unless the visitor wished to speak with them as well. Often, these visitors were asked to join the family for a meal before heading back out into their travels. During these meals, stories were swapped, and laughter filled the air. As the visitor left, they were followed by a chorus to come again any time, and they echoed by extending their own invitation to those they visited.

Children were taught from a young age how to socialize. They were sent outside to make their own friends, and taught how to be self sufficient. This gave them the confidence to speak to others. In school, they were instructed on what was appropriate conversation, and what was not. Children were often taught not to speak unless spoken to. This was to teach them not to interrupt those that were talking, and to truly listen to those around them. They were not taught to listen to make a reply, but were taught to listen so they could learn. This made them become friendly, and compassionate adults that were able to hold efficient conversation in the highest of social settings. Even home schooled children were taught how to behave when company was over, and were taught social cues by their parents. This was important, because even the most basic of farmers were visited often by the mayor of the town, or the pastor, and if the family, or even the children did not know how to socialize, it was an embarrassment. Of course, people were understanding, but conversation was key to survival, and if you were not good at communicating, it could sometimes be hard for someone to understand you, and children were taught this so they would take their social lessons seriously.

Strangers were welcomed with open arms as well. There was not a stigma that strangers were a bad thing, as you couldn't make friends if you weren't nice to strangers. Talking to even the oddest of strangers was a breeze. If a new person rode into town, they were welcomed into the home by the mayor or local pastor depending on the jurisdiction of the town. Sometimes even the sheriff invited the stranger over to his house. They person was treated like family, and served a fine feast to replenish their energy from their long journey, and that dinner was spent conversing about life, and getting to know this stranger. By the end of the evening, generally the house was filled with laughter as stories were swapped like they had been friends since birth. Strangers were not made to feel uncomfortable, or like an outsider. If the stranger had a trade, they were sent on to the local person who was an expert on the trade for an internship or to help and expand the knowledge about the subject. If there was no one who was an expert in that trade, this person was set up with help to start it up if they planned to stay in town long. Drifters were even more highly revered, as they had so many stories of different places they had been, and often he would spend his time in the town at various houses as he told his tales over and over again, entertaining the locals, and getting room and board and food for doing nothing more than telling stories of the places he had been.

People gathered together all of the time. Most weekends were filled with gatherings of friends and family, and even some nights during the week there were people gathering together for fun and festivity. Women regularly gathered in what were called knitting circles, where they would swap project and techniques, and have tea. They chatted about their weeks as they knitted, crocheted or stitched together. Young ladies were brought up in these environments as well, and they learned not only valuable skills, but how to speak and act like ladies. When in a social setting, the ladies were very eloquent, and well made up. Every social setting was a reason to look their best, and they made sure that they did.

Acquaintances that met on the street would stop and chat with each other. Even if they were in a hurry, they were never in too much of a hurry to stop and say a quick hello, and extend an invitation to stop by the house sometime. This way of life made even people you didn't know that well feel like family. You treated everyone with the respect you wish you received, and in return that respect was bestowed upon you. Communicating with your neighbors, and inviting people into your home meant that they would be more willing to do the same for you. Even acquaintances were often seen mingling together, just like the best of friends.

People that did not live in town were no less social, as they still had to make regular trips into town to buy the necessities they could not make themselves. These trips were treated as an all day event. The night before they were to set off into town, they bathed and went to bed earlier than usual.

Then they were up before the sun the next day and they hitched up the horses to the wagon and headed into town wearing their best clothes. Once in town, they visited the store first, to ensure that they had what they needed. They only picked up the textiles they needed to make the things they needed at home, and since they had no refrigeration in that time period, they did not have to worry about anything spoiling. If there was any money left over, the children would be allowed to buy some candy, often having to share, but since a penny would fill a bag, there was not much worry about anyone feeling left out. Often, if the family didn't have money to get their kids some candy, and the shopkeeper knew they were from the rural areas, he would give the children a few pieces free of charge. The children would then thank the shopkeeper with a sincere gratitude, and savor their candies, often making them stretch for several days. After their store visit, they would go to visit some friends and family that lived in town. They often would be invited for meals at various people's homes. Back then it was considered very rude to not offer a meal to a visitor, and it was even more rude to turn down a meal without a valid reason. However, even if you just ate at someone else's house, you would be fed a light snack at the current place you were at. Famine was considered the only excuse not to eat at someone's house as you would not want to deplete someone else's rations.

After a supper at their last stop for the day in town, the adults would chat as the children played, and got well worn out. This was one of the few times that children could stay up with the adults, and were allowed to be outside well after dark. If it was a nice night, often the adults would gather out under the stars and watch the children frolic about and enjoy the evening. Finally, well after sun down, they family would pack back into the wagon, and head home. After unloading their items from the store, they would head to bed, anxiously anticipating the next time they could make a trip into town. The children would go to sleep dreaming about the day's events, and the adults would sleep well, thoroughly exhausted from the adventure they had that day.

As crazy as this all seems, if you read any Laura Ingalls Wilder book, you will find these events to be true. Life was a simpler time then in some ways. Though there was more work to be done, it was easier to enjoy it knowing that you could look forward to something every day, and never knowing when a visitor was going to stop by put mystery in every single day.

So what happened? It seems like things today have made a complete one hundred and eighty degree turn from where things used to be. We are going in the opposite direction from where we used to be, and yet we claim that it is all for peace and acceptance. People are so closed off, and they never really talk to anyone. That is the saddest thing to see in all honesty.

Take a walk outside. How many people would you see? One? Two? Or would you even see any? Once upon a time, the whole block would be alight with people out chatting. Now it is always almost dead. People stay inside, and hide behind their fancy screens, and their technology. Children rarely go outdoors, unless they have old fashioned parents.

The media portrays the darkness of the world, filled with violence and fear. Children are shooting up schools rather than making friends. That is majorly contributed to by the fact that bullies are everywhere. The neighborly friends with anyone vibe has completely disappeared. If anyone drops by someone's house unannounced, they are met with the double barrel of a shot gun aimed at their face, rather than welcomed inside. Trips into town are hurried, as people just want to get the necessities and head back home to sit in front of the television. No one drops by friend's houses any more. If it can be avoided, they don't even leave the house. A lot of people now just order what they need and have it delivered overnight to their house. You can even do your grocery shopping this way.

Friendships have changed as well. It used to be if you saw your friend in the street, you greeted them with enthusiasm. Now it seems people hide from those that they know to avoid having to spend prolonged time in public. This causes those that they know to feel offended, yet simultaneously relieved, then abhorred that they feel relieved, so they take it out on the person who avoided them, and that is how anger and resentment breeds.

Dinner invitations are very rare, even when people have company over. The company is ushered out before a meal happens, so people can avoid having to offer a meal to their company. Rare dinner invitations are planned out weeks in advance, and often canceled last minute. No one sits around the table and shares stories anymore, unless it is a holiday that they have to attend. Children are not even sent outside to play with the neighborhood kids. They have strict play dates set up, and are not allowed outside unless they are supervised inside a fenced in yard.

Children are not taught how to be civilized in public either. All manners classes have been removed from schools, and are rarely taught at home. Children do not get to spend time learning how to behave, and how to hold a proper conversation in every day life. This leads to them growing up unsure of how to approach people. This causes a great dip in respect for others. It is only getting worse.

Drifters are now treated like lepers. People no longer sit in awe of their wondrous stories, instead, they are treated like dirt. This is because people can just do a quick search on the internet about all the places this person has been, and rather than listen to a human tell the tale, they would rather read about it from the web. That way they don't have to waste their food and space on some stranger. This aloof way that they are treated has lead to a stigma that homeless people are horrible, and that is the farthest from the truth.

Go down any New York street, and you will see people hustling and bustling about, and thousands of people pressed together, but they never acknowledge each other, unless it is to say something rude. They all have frowns on their faces, and rarely look up from their phones, or whatever it may be that they are doing. A person that waves is laughed at or scorned. There are so many people, and it is so full of hate, and rudeness, that it is better to just keep your mouth shut and stay inside.

The world has become a silent, sullen place. With how angry it has become it is no wonder why so many people have trouble talking with others. So do not feel alone, the entire world seems to have some semblance of a problem with communication, which makes it even harder for those with social anxiety or extreme shyness to talk to anyone that they do not know extremely well.

Possible Causes

There are many possible causes for this silence struck pandemic. Most of it can be attributed to one or more of the many technological advances that we have seen over the years. No one person has been able to pinpoint exactly what it is that has changed the amicable ways of the world. Here are some of the possible causes, and you can try to decide for yourself what you think has been the downfall of communication.

- The Telephone: The invention of the telephone made it easier to take the human element out of a conversation. Instead of going to someone's house every so often and staying a few hours, and having a meal, they could call to say what needed to be said, and then cut the conversation short with the excuse that they were wracking up too many minutes that month. They didn't have to stay on the phone yacking for hours on end, because generally, the person on the other end of the line agreed and hung up as well.

  The telephone, back when it was invented, was so expensive that only the rich people, and government agencies owned them. Invented in nineteen eighty nine by Alexander Graham-Bell, it was the most technologically advanced thing since the dawn of electricity. In the beginning, it cost over a thousand dollars to own a single phone. To make a call, Bell Telephone Industries charged a dollar a minute to dispatch that call. That was a lot of money considering the average worker was lucky to make fifty cents an hour. One minute call time would have been two hours wages, so most average wage households did not have a telephone in the house. That was until the mid nineteen hundreds, after Henry Ford invented the concept of mass production. A company made a telephone that was way cheaper than Bell Industries ancient phone design, and they found a better way to dispatch calls to make the calls cheaper. During this time, wages went up a lot as well. By this time the minimum wage was about two dollars an hour. This made phones more common in average households. By the nineteen seventies, a home phone was a staple in each household, and calls only cost ten cents a minute. This was a great thing, as by this time, wages were up to seven dollars an hour for minimum wage. The company that was instrumental in lowering the price of the phone? Well it is known today as AT&T.

Due to its cost, the telephone may not have been the

downfall of modern communication, but it definitely could have had a hand in it. Especially as it became easier, and cheaper to purchase. People called rather than stopped by, and these calls did not have to drone on and on, as time was money. This allowed conversation to become shorter, and it made its way into everyday life as well.

- Television: The television was a lot cheaper than the telephone was. It was also a way to get the news a lot easier, as you didn't have to wait until a friend heard something and get back to you. There were also some good programs to watch during the day that entertained people. This entertainment made them want to stay inside, and watch it all day. Well the adults at least. Children were still sent outside to play.

The original television was black and white and only had three channels. It was small, and could sit on the dining room table. Brand new, they cost about three hundred dollars, and they had really long rabbit ear antennas. At the beginning, this was the only option you had, but as time went on, there were bigger console televisions available. Eventually, the color television was introduced, and some time after that, more channels were added, as cable became a thing. More and more time was spent inside watching TV. Not just by adults anymore, either. Children were inside more often and watched shows that were geared towards their age groups. People went out and mingled with their neighbors less and less.

Television alone probably was not the downfall of the communication era, but it was a precedent to it. A lot of people began staying inside to watch their soaps instead of going outside to spend time with actual people. For the longest time, children were still sent out to play while the parents watched TV, but as the parents moved to colored cable, the children got the still working black and white rabbit eared television, and the trend progressed as in the older days, television sets lasted forever.

- Game Consoles: Today there are several hi-tech game consoles out ther for people to choose from, and they are often played for hours on end, while the player ignores the outside world. Back when they were first invented, they were a lot different, but no less desirable. They were the envy of every household, and a child that had one was instantly popular, but he never used that popularity because he was too busy inside playing his new game. When the original Atari came out, it was the sensation that swept the nation.

  The first ever game console was nothing like the ones we have today. They took a lot more effort to play. To make a single move, you had to write a program first. This was difficult, but the kids in those days didn't mind, as to them it was a game console, and that was the coolest thing they had ever seen. They also learned about computer programming before home computers were a thing. As time progressed, the programs were written into the game at production, so all kids had to do was play the game. They also went from almost fifteen hundred dollars to a hundred and fifty dollars. While that was still pretty expensive, it was a lot more affordable than the Atari. The most popular and innovative of these new consoles? The Nintendo Entertainment System, or NES for short. It was the console that every kid wanted, and most kids were able to get for Christmas or their birthday. With the debut of the game Super Mario Brothers steppong away from the normal games of Pong and Galactia, this thrilling console had kids of all ages, and even adults gathered around it to enjoy it. This further engulfed them into their anti-social bubbles as they were too engrossed in the games to go outside.

Video Games are blamed by many as being the downfall of modern society. That can be kind of seen as accurate, as there were so many people beginning to stay indoors rather than going outside. However, there were plenty of friendly people left in the world, and people still visited one another, so is this really the truth? Maybe as they progressed, but it was not an immediate destruction.

- Media: This one can be brutal. People are so easily influenced by the media, that they could tell the people that Donald Trump farted unicorns, and they would almost believe it. Okay, maybe not that bad, but that is the general idea with the media. Nowadays, the media is filled with bombings, kidnappings and other fear mongering materials that it makes it hard to trust the people around you.

  In the beginning, the news just stated that. The news. It gave news of the war if there was one, and news With all the fear inducing news, it makes it hard to want to even talk to anyone, because it seems as if everyone is a murderer now. This is not a conducive environment from the friendly ways of the past.

Media could be considered the downfall of the friendly atmosphere, as it seeds fear of the human race in your mind, and that is what seems to have closed people off from their natural chatty instincts.

- Internet: The dawn of the internet saw a rise in introverts massively. It is no secret that the internet has taken over the minds of most of our youth. This goes hand in hand with the media, as it is the main source of all media output.

So those are some of the possible causes of why it is harder now to talk to people than it used to be. Of course, for some people it is harder than others. People with anxiety, or shyness have a hard time even talking to people that are deemed safe by people they trust. It isn't really caused by fear, just a nervousness that causes these people to clam up. Chances are, since you are reading this, you are one of these people.

Do not fret. This book will help you get through this.

However, be prepared. Sometimes it takes more than self

help, and if your problem has deeper seated issues, you may want to get the help of a psychiatrist. If these tips do not help, it is best to seek the help of one if you wish to be more of a conversationalist, and it is essential for your mental and emotional health. There will be more on that at the end of this book.

Chapter 2

Secret Tips 1-2

Step One-Talking to Yourself

This may seem a little silly, but it really does help. Actually it is the easiest way to get over your shyness, as it is more awkward to talk to yourself than it is to talk to other people. You just have to get past the first hump of not wanting to look like a fool, and own it.

Go into a room with a mirror, start by offering your hand to shake and mime shaking hands with the person staring back at you while introducing yourself. This may feel a little weird, as there is not going to be a meeting of hands, due to you only having the conversation with yourself.

Once you get past the standard greeting it is time to hold a conversation. You can either say your mirrored self's responses or you can keep them in your head. This is where it can get tricky. You cannot think of specific to you answers, rather, you have to think of general answers, as you are not really the person you are talking to. Talk away as if there was an actual person holding a conversation with you. You can think of this as a live diary, but more civilized and social, as you don't want to spill your secrets to someone who is essentially standing in as a stranger.

Here is a little scenario to help you visualize what it would be like.

SCENARIO

Kelly had just finished reading *How to Talk to Anyone: Ten Secrets You Wish You Knew*, and she wanted to try out the first tip, which was called "Talking to Yourself". She stepped into her bathroom, and closed the door.

"Okay Kelly. You can do this. You have to become better at holding conversation, as your husband's job requires you to attend various social events with him."

Looking into the mirror she offered her hand to the cold glass, feeling slightly foolish.

"Hello, my name is Kelly. And you are?"

In her head, she planned the response.

I am Richard Simms. Pleasure to meet you, Kelly. She used her husband's boss's name as that was the one she was sure she knew.

"Pleasure to meet you too, sir. How are you and your wife and kids?"

They are doing well, as am I. How about your children?

"Oh no children yet sir. Wanting to get ahead financially first."

A great plan, I must say. Children are very expensive little buggers.

Kelly was interrupted then, as her husband walked into the

bathroom.

"Who on Earth are you talking to?"

"I am practicing holding a conversation. I don't want to embarrass you tomorrow at the banquet." Kelly blushed.

"Awe, sweetheart, you could never embarrass me, but I appreciate the effort, and I am glad you are taking the steps necessary to better yourself. I am proud of you." Her husband kissed her forehead and left.

After that boost of confidence, Kelly found it much easier to practice her conversation skills, and felt less awkward about talking to herself in the mirror.

It may seem a little awkward to talk to yourself in a mirror, but after awhile it will be much easier, as you will start to feel better about helping yourself become the best that you can be. If someone comes in and asks you what you are doing, explain to them what you are trying to do. You never know, maybe they will try it for themselves.

Of course there is still a stigma that talking to yourself means that you are crazy, but once you explain that you are not trying to be weird, you just are trying to become better at conversation, people will understand. It is getting harder and harder for people to hold a normal conversation in this world, so it is always refreshing to hear that someone is trying to better themselves.

Step Two- Have a Few Ice Breakers

It is no secret that after the initial introductions conversation gets really awkward if there are no real conversation starters in the room. You say hello, state your name, and ask a few questions about what the person does, and how their day has been, but after that is over, this is when conversation dies out with a bunch of "Ums" and "Uhhh". Having a few ice breakers is always important as you can keep the conversation going, and often have a few laughs going at the end.

Of course it is hard to tell exactly what you should use as an ice breaker, and that is why most people have a hard time keeping the conversation going. However there are few fool proof ice breakers that will make talking to someone a breeze. This section will go over some ice breakers to use... and some to avoid.

Good Ice Breakers

- Latest viral cat video: Pretty much everyone in the world loves cat videos, and a lot of people have seen them. Bringing that up in conversation is always a great way to push conversation along. It is a safe topic that won't offend people, and if someone hasn't seen the video, you can show it to them, eliciting a few laughs and smiles. Almost everyone loves cat videos.

- Food: Everyone eats. So ask the person what kind of food they like. It is always pertinent to ask them first, because if they are vegan, you don't want to say "Bacon is the greatest, is it not?" Discuss different cuisines, and if they have not tried one of your favorites, suggest a good place to find it. Talking about food can bring people closer together, as they find common likes and interests in cuisines.

- Music: Everyone listens to music. No matter what their tastes, everyone loves music. You cannot deny the fact that life would be boring without it. It fills the awkward silences, and it can bring up someone who is down. There is no escaping the fact that music is tied to emotions as well. Try asking the person what their favorite song is. Ask them the genres they like. If you find you have some interests that are similar, that is great, and that will further boost the conversation.

- Hobbies: Everyone has a passion that probably has nothing to do with their job. Hobbies are what make life interesting. It is a safe topic to approach, because many people love to talk about what they enjoy, but rarely anyone asks.

- Anything to do with interests: Pretty much anything to do with personal interests is safe to talk about, because people love to talk about themselves. They love to make known what they enjoy, and they love when someone shows interest in them. However, most people are too shy to actually talk about themselves unprompted because they do not wish to seem conceited.

Bad Ice Breakers

- Politics: There are so many different opinions out there, and unfortunately with politics, everyone thinks that they are right. The conversation can get really awkward if you are a Democrat butting heads with a Republican. That is only the tip of the iceberg though. Tempers often flare at the slightest mention that either party may be corrupt, so it is best all around to just avoid the conversation entirely.
- Religion: This is another one that is best avoided. Religion is a very sensitive subject for some, and no one wants someone else's religion shoved in their

faces. That is why you are better off keeping this one put away.

- Life choices: It is great that you have decided to become a vegan and all, but you do not have to convert everyone who is around you. Same with any of the life choices you make, whether you sell avon or those scammy weight loss products, pretty much no one wants to hear the spiel. Save it for if you are asked.

So there you have it. Some good, and bad, icebreakers to help you extend any conversation past the initial hello. Once you are able to establish a gateway to conversation, you will be able to carry on a lot easier than you would if you had not used an ice breaker at all, and were floundering about like a fish out of water, trying to figure out what to say.

How These Tips Help

These tips help you relax a little bit. They give you a little confidence boost, knowing that you are prepared to hold a conversation with people you may meet, because you have practiced the basics. It is a lot easier to do something once you have practiced it a few times.

It also helps you get past the awkwardness, as nothing is more awkward than holding a conversation with yourself. You will be able to talk to someone without feeling silly, because you couldn't possibly feel any more goofy than you did talking to a mirror.

Follow these tips to get the ball rolling on talking to people.

Chapter 3

Secret Tips 3-4

Now that you have gotten past the tips on how to approach and talk to someone, it is time to move on to the tips on how to hold a conversation. This is important, because starting a conversation is only a small part of the battle. This means that you have to be able to continue a conversation past the point of the ice breaker.

Conversations do not have to be hours long but you do have to keep them at a length that does not make you seem rude, or disinterested. If you only talk to someone about one subject and then leave, the person will feel as if they did something to offend you or something like that. You do not want to leave anyone feeling that way.

The best way to avoid that is to make sure that you keep the conversation going to the point where it would be safe to exit without offending the person you are talking too. This section will help you more understand how to keep a conversation going, and keep it going well.

Tip Three- Self Disclosure

To truly understand this tip, there is going to have to be some in depth explanation of what self disclosure is. To save you from having to look it up, this tip will include all the information you need to know about it. Of course that will make this tip a lot longer, but it is better to have a long tip that you understand, than a short briefing on something that leaves you confused.

Self disclosure is where you add to a conversation by giving the other person information about yourself. This is a hard thing to do, as most people worry about boring others with talk of themselves, or they are afraid to seem conceited.

There are two dimensions to self disclosure. They are breadth and depth. These are both essential to holding a good conversation, and connecting with the person you are talking to. You want to be able to connect with the people around you or else you will not be able to hold a true and meaningful conversation. You have to have both to truly enable the act of self disclosure.

Breadth of self disclosure refers to the range of topics you discuss when opening up about yourself. No you don't have to disclose your deepest darkest secrets, but giving someone a little bit of information about several different subjects about yourself allows them to feel a little closer to you, thus allowing them to open up about themselves. This helps extend the conversation and lets the person feel values, as if you really are interested in talking with them. Try starting with the easiest topics, such as interests, and move on to schooling, and views on the world. The more subjects you cover, the longer the conversation will be, and the more you will be able to connect with the person you are talking too.

Depth is slightly more difficult to reach. Now if you are just chatting up with someone you don't plan to develop a deep friendship with, you can almost skip depth, but a deep conversation is needed for those you wish to establish a true friendship with. However, even in a simple conversation, you need to have some depth to what you are saying. Tell them about the time you broke your arm in third grade, or something of the like. Give them a memory to really make them feel as if you care about the conversation you are having, and are not just shooting the breeze to pass time.

The act of self disclosure is a type of social penetration. This is a theory that you can only establish any type of relationship, whether it be romantic or platonic, by communication. But not just any type of communication, systematically fluid conversation. This means that over time, you let the person in more and more,and you change the direction of your conversation regularly to establish a connection with the person you are communicating with.

You also have to allow time for the person to reciprocate in the conversation. Don't spend the entire time talking about yourself. If you are worried about droning on too long about what you like and such, try employing the one detail method. This means that you share a detail about yourself, and let the other person share a detail about themselves. Continue this on until you find a happy medium between not sharing enough and talking too much.

As you can see self disclosure is very important, as you need to really allow a person to feel as if you are invested in the conversation. If you do not seem like you really care to talk to them, they will close off, and not want to talk much more than the basic hello followed by an ice breaker subject. So how do you efficiently employ this technique?

- Start Small: On top of them feeling like you are interested, they also have to be interested in what you have to say. Rather than unloading a whole pile of information on someone that doesn't really care, start with a small bit of information to see if they take the bait. If you use the icebreaker about music, try telling them your favorite song, and explaining a basic reason for why you love it. If they just give you a one word reply, it is best to duck out of the conversation then. They don't really care. However, if they seem interested, and ask you more then you can start talking about more of your interests and such.

- Decide on The Type of Conversation: You should always try to approach every conversation as if you are trying to make a new friend. However, if you are at a convention with people from around the globe, chances are you are not going to establish a life long friendship. You should still show interest in the person, but that would definitely impact the type of information that you are going to divulge. You don't want someone you are never going to see again knowing a deep secret about you. Instead tell them about childhood memories that you don't feel would impact how they think of you. Your favorite thing to do as a child or things like that. Those are safe subjects for people who you are just talking to in that moment.

- Skim the Surface: You want people to be interested in you for a long time. This means that you cannot divulge everything about you in one conversation. You have to be conservative with your information. The best way to do this is to take a little bit of information from many different subjects to talk about. As you get to know a person more and more, you can add more information to that. This helps you also ensure that you are not talking about yourself too much.

- Allow Reciprocation: The best part of self disclosure is that it allows the other person a gateway to talk about themselves as well. You don't want to hog the stage and only talk about yourself. You want to keep the flow of information even. Give the other person some time to tell you about themselves as well. Conversation will come alight as you are swapping stories and some fun little tidbits of information about yourself.

- Be Loose: Telling someone about yourself should be done with ease. You don't want to sound like someone who is selling something, though in reality that is what you are doing in a way. You are trying to convince the person to like you with the truth. However, it should not sound like you are a documentary. You should be light and airy when talking about yourself. Make the person interested. Intrigue them, and draw them in, make them want to know more about you.

- Timing: Just like when you deliver the punchline to a joke, it is all about the timing. You have to time the information that you deliver. This is a little tricky if you don't know what goes into timing a deliverance. There has to be a level of interest from the other person. To ensure that you have their interest, you have to make them ask a few questions. You can't just offer up all the information. However, you can't make them pry every bit of info from you either. There has to be a give and take kind of flow going on there.

- Caution: There are some things that you do not tell a person you just met. It may seem like you have known the person forever, but you still have to use caution when divulging certain things. For example, if you were a former addict, it is best to not mention it unless absolutely necessary. You do not want anything to skew how they think of you until they get to know you. If you are confident in yourself however, then try divulging that info. What you are cautious with depends on you.

There you have it. Self disclosure at its finest. This is one of the most important things to holding a good conversation. Now remember, your entire conversation does not have to consist of self disclosure alone, but throwing in a few facts here and there go a long way. Make sure you utilize this to the fullest advantage possible.

Tip Four- Engage the Other Person Fully

Part of the problem these days is that conversation becomes one sided. Even though both parties are speaking, they are not really in the conversation. They are not properly engaging the other person. This is a big issue, when conversation relies entirely on both parties being actively engaged in the conversation to allow it to succeed. If you are not actively engaging the other person, and not engaged yourself, then you will fall flat in the conversation.

First off, how you can be engaged in the conversation better, without taking it over.

- Actively Listen: No one wants to feel like they are talking to a brick wall. They want to feel like the person they are talking to is genuinely interested in what they have to say. This means that you have to listen to understand. Today's generation teaches you to listen to reply, and that is where the problem lies. By only listening to reply, you are not processing what they person is saying, because your mind is on yourself. This is a selfish, bad habit that this day and age has taken to sticking too.

- Reply with Interest: Even if you are not quite interested in what the other person is talking about, you should always reply with interest. It is polite, and even though you may not be interested in it now, you might gain some interesting knowledge by listening to what they have to say. You can't just expect everyone to have the same interests as you, and there are probably things that you like that others do not like but they still act like they are at least interested in it, because it is the polite thing to do.

- Ask Questions: Asking questions to get more information about what they are talking about shows the other person that you were listening, and that you want to know more. It allows the person to be relieved, because then they do not feel like they are boring you with their information. The only way that they know that you are interested is if you are asking questions. Then they know that it is okay to continue talking about the subject they are on.

- Be THERE: I know it can be hard if someone is droning on and on about something that you have no interest in, but it is still good etiquette to be there mentally. This means that when someone is talking, don't let your mind go on vacation, and tune the person out, because if you are that disinterested in them it is more polite to change the subject rather than just leave the conversation mentally.

That is how you can be engaged in a conversation. Following these tips will allow you to breathe easier knowing that you are pleasantly talking to a person, and you wont offend them because you seem disinterested. You just have to practice these things, because sometimes it can be a little difficult.

How to Engage Them

- Be Interesting: This does not mean you have to make up stories. It has nothing to do with the information you are giving at all. You just have to deliver it in an interesting way. You could tell someone you climbed mount Everest on the back of Dwayne Johnson, and if you tell the story in a monotone voice, it will sound boring. It is not what you are saying, it is how you are saying. Tell them your stories as if you were telling them for the first time. Be engaged yourself, and show the person that you want them to talk to you. You want their attention. Only then will you get the attention you so desire.

- Leave Openings: Even without using self disclosure, you still have to leave openings for the other person to talk, no matter the subject. No one wants to stand there and listen to someone take control of the conversation. You might as well be talking to yourself for that matter. Or to the plant in the corner. You have to let the other person talk as well. A good conversation allows both parties to talk equally, and without any hitches. It is not one person talking about everything while the other person stands there and nods.

- Allow Questions: If a person asks a question, don't dodge it. This should not have to be said, but a lot of people dodge questions for fear of sounding conceited, but in truth you just seem rude. If someone is asking a question, you are not going to sound conceited by answering it. If you dodge a question, the person will feel as if they offended you, and they will be less likely to stay engaged in the conversation.

That is how you engage someone in conversation. It is a lot easier than staying engaged in a conversation as long as they are interested in what is being said. All you have to do is be open and friendly, and let the rest fall into place.

How These Tips Help

These tips are designed to help you keep a conversation

going without being nervous. These tips also help improve your communication skills. By using these tips you will feel more comfortable having a longer conversation with someone that you just met, than you would be if you were just trying to find things to talk about.

These tips will give you the boost you need to feel confident in your abilities to talk to people and really enjoy the conversation without having to worry every second that you are saying something wrong.

Chapter 4

Secret Tips 5-6

These tips are for what you should do during and after a conversation with someone. They are tips on how to properly act when communicating, as there is often some confusion on what to do. Especially now that it is no longer a curriculum at school or home. Do not fret. This book will clarify that right up.

Tip Five- Etiquette During a Convo

It is of utmost importance that you have the proper etiquette when talking to someone. The key to holding a good conversation is to not offend them, and to show them that you are a good person to talk to. You want to hold their attention and let them know that they have yours. Otherwise you will not get very far in the communication realm, as people will not want to talk to you, thinking you are rude.

So it is best to study up on proper etiquette before you put yourself out there. While most of these are common sense, they are in here just in case nerves cause a problem with combining common sense with communication. That is a real problem a lot of people have. They cannot rely on their common sense because they are too nervous to remember to use it.

So here are the etiquette rules to help you out. Remember, a slip up is okay as long as you don't do it continually, but it is best to try to be as clean cut as possible to avoid any issues.

- Handshake: This is the first thing you should do, as you say hello. Unless the person is germaphobic, or you are, not offering a handshake is considered rude. If you do have a phobia of germs, it is best to explain that as you are saying hello, so there are no misunderstandings. Make sure that they know that you are still pleased to meet them, you just would rather not shake their hand. Most people can be pretty understanding.

  The perfect handshake is firm, but pliant. You can't grip too tight, because you are not trying to intimidate someone, and a grip too loose makes people feel that you are not that thrilled to meet them, and are only doing so out of necessity. This is not a great first impression, as people want to feel like they are worth getting to know. So it is best to make sure you give a good, true handshake.

- Eye Contact: This one is important to maintain from the beginning to end. It is always disconcerting to talk to someone who is looking off in the distance or anywhere else but who is talking to them. (autistic people are not counted in this, nor are the ocularly impaired) Eye contact shows that you are paying attention to them. To show you why eye contact is so important, let us have a mini history lesson.

Back in the time of extreme social hierarchy, where people who made less money than you were deemed undesirable, eye contact was a way of establishing that social ladder. Anyone who was deemed below you had to make eye contact with you, while you were not to make eye contact with them. To make eye contact with a person deemed lowly, put you on their level, and could cause you to lose your social position if caught.

Kings never looked anyone but other kings in the eye, no one ever made eye contact with serfs other than other serfs. Men did not make eye contact with women, as even women were deemed below them. They only time someone made eye contact with a woman that was not another woman, was a servant, or a peasant to a duchess or queen. Eye contact was the main factor of social hierachy

By not looking someone in the eye during conversation, you are essentially saying that they are beneath you, and that what they have to say is not important. That may not be what you are trying to do, but that is the message you are portraying when you refuse to look someone in the eye.

- Body Language: This will be more brushed on in a later chapter, but it also falls under etiquette. You have to have an open body language in a conversation, otherwise you risk making a person feel as if you are unapproachable, and not open to conversation. You can also make them feel as if what they are saying has no value. You can do so much damage with a few simple gestures, and this is a problem. You have to be careful with your stance and make sure that you are not closing yourself off.

- No Phone: This should go without saying, but if your phone goes off, DON'T ANSWER IT! Society today is so caught up in the conversations that they have going on on the other side of the screen, that they forget the importance of conversation with the person on the other side of the table. You are in a real time conversation with a real person. (Not that the person texting you isn't real, but they are not there.) The best thing to do is to put your phone on silent if you know you are going to talk to people. That way you do not feel tempted to pull it out and text rather than talking to those around you.

Cell phones are a wonderfully destructive device. They can help you connect with people from around the world, but unfortunately that causes you to disconnect from the people that are right next to you. A lot of people use their phone as a crutch to not have to talk to people when they feel uncomfortable. This does not help you in any way. They only way to become comfortable with a situation is to put yourself out there, and talk to people. Find someone to talk to and eventually you will take your mind off of the fact that you are anxious about being around people.

- Don't Interrupt: When someone is talking to you, it is best to stay quiet until you are sure they have finished what they are saying. You have to be very careful when talking to someone that you are listening to them, and not listening to respond. This is one of the biggest problem in today's conversations. No one listens to people for more than knowing when to jump in and reply. This leads to more people interrupting, which often angers the other person, and makes them not want to talk to you any longer.

  Listen to the person, and remember that you would not want to be interrupted. No one likes to be talked over, and no one likes talking to someone who constantly does it. Be patient. Your time to talk will come.

- Personal Space: This is a big one. A lot of people get really close to people when they are talking. This is uncomfortable for the other person. You have to make sure that you keep a good distance between you and the other person. Arm's length apart is generally a good chatting distance unless you are in a loud place, and then from forearm length apart is generally as close as you should be. If it is too loud to hear then, maybe hold the conversation until you are in a quieter environment.

  Claustrophobia is a big problem for a large majority of a population. Invading someone's personal space can make them very uncomfortable. You have to respect that people need personal space when talking to you. Even if they don't have claustrophobia, it is still gross when someone is so close to you that you can feel their spit as they are talking. Keep the distance.

- Get Close: This may seem contradicting to the last statement, but you have to be close enough that it does not look like you are trying to escape the conversation. However, it is not that contradictory. You just have to find a happy medium. You want to be close enough that the other person is not sniffing themselves trying to figure out if it is them, but you have to be far enough away that you are not crowding their personal space.

A good indicator is your arms. Of course you do not physically stretch them out to see if you are standing close enough, but rather you visualize where you are at. You should never so close that you have to bend your arm at more than a ninety degree angle to touch them, but you should not be so far away that when your arms are fully outstretched your palms can't rest on their shoulders. Try to stay in that golden circle of space, and you should be good.

Those are the tips for etiquette during a conversation. Follow these, and you should have no problem with people not wanting to talk to you. You will make the other person feel respected, and that is what you are striving for.

Tip Six- Etiquette When Leaving a Conversation

- Timing: As stated before, timing is everything when talking to people. You have to be good at your timing and actually know when to say something when not to say something. In this case, timing has to do with when to exit a conversation. No matter how good a conversation has been, you begin to wear out your welcome. If a person starts to look around or shift about, they are probably ready to go, or do something else. This is your cue to end the conversation if they do not. Finish what you were saying, and then use an exit phrase such as "Oh I can't believe how much of your time I have taken! It was so great talking to you I just got swept up in the moment!" Make them feel good while ending the conversation.

- Ending Phrase: As mentioned in the above bullet, you have to use a good ending phrase to make the person feel as if the conversation ending is not their fault, even if it is. Be polite, and make them feel like you were so enthralled by talking to them that you regret having to end the conversation, but you do not want to take up any more of their time. This will make them feel valued, and that will make them want to talk to you again.

- Ask for Contact Info: If you have the chance of seeing someone again, or just would like to stay in touch, ask if they would like to exchange contact information. If they say yes, go ahead and give them your number and ask for theirs, giving a test call to make sure you input the number right, and allowing them to be sure of the same, as the will have your number from the call. If they do not wish to exchange information, do not push. It doesn't mean you did anything wrong, they just may not think that they will see you again. That is okay.

Always ask if they want to exchange information. It is a lot more comfortable for them, as it gives them a little more room to say no without feeling bad. Asking them for their contact information directly does not allow for them to say no without feeling bad, because you assumed that they wanted to. Remember, good conversation does not mean they have to become your best friend. A lot of people become so attached to someone they had a single enthralling conversation with, that they are upset when the person does not want to keep in touch. This is simple human nature, as we are designed to communicate for survival. Breaking yourself of this habit will be difficult, but if you do it, you will be less affected by the rejection you feel when someone does not wish to stay in touch.

- Follow Up: This only refers to people who exchanged info. If they give you their contact information, then text or call them the next day to see how they are doing and let them know that you were serious about wanting to stay in touch. Make the person feel important, but only text once, and let them respond.

They might be busy when you try to reach them, and will get back to you later.

These are the etiquette rules for ending a conversation. If you use them, you can be confident that you are not leaving someone with awkwardness in the air.

How These Tips Help

These tips give you the boost up in a conversation to show a person that you are respectful, and that you have proper manners. This will make them enjoy talking to you a lot better than if you did not know these rules.

Etiquette is slowly slipping away, by trying to bring it back, you will also start a ripple effect, as the person you are talking to will pick up on these social cues, and start using them in their conversations with others. By doing this little simple thing, you can help bring proper conversation etiquette back into a trend.

Chapter 5

Secret Tips 7-10

These tips are just extra tips that you should know and insert throughout different conversations. They do not necessarily have to apply to every conversation, as they are not about the conversation itself, but how to psych yourself up to talk to people, and how to handle rejection without letting it ruin you.

Tip Seven- Get Out of Your Head

You have to get out of your own head to ever hold a good conversation with someone, because you have to be able to approach someone to talk to them. If you are stuck in your head, and the "Oh I can't" thoughts, then you will be stuck at only talking to people you have to.

By getting out of your head, you will feel confident enough to approach a person that you have never met before, and that has no correlation to any of your friends. This is the best feeling, knowing that you can make friends anywhere, and not have to worry about going somewhere and not knowing anyone there.

Imagine you are going to a party. Your friend says that they will meet you there. You are glad, because you don't know anyone else who will be attending, or they are just minor acquaintances from work or school. You get there, and your friend texts you saying that they can't come because something came up. You don't panic because you decide to just go find someone to talk to. You walk up to a guy or girl you have never seen before, and strike up a conversation. Before the night is up, you have met seven new people that you really get along with.

That is what can happen once you stop the thoughts that you aren't good enough to talk to someone, or that you are too boring for anyone to want to talk to. Confidence is key. Boost yourself up, and as they say, fake it till you make it. You have to boost yourself up, because there is not going to be anyone in the world who is able to make you feel better about yourself than you can. Go in with the mindset that you are worth talking to, and that you are funny, and witty. By believing in yourself, people will be more open to you, as they can see that you are confident in yourself.

Tip Eight- Boost Your Self Esteem

This one goes hand in hand with getting out of your head. You have to believe in yourself to get out of your head. If you have low self esteem, you will be more prone to rejection, because just like lions, people can pick out the meek ones. No one wants to have to carry the entire conversation, so they generally steer away from the shy people, and gravitate to someone who they know will actively engage in conversation.

The way to boost your self esteem can also involve a mirror. Stand in front of it for ten minutes a day only saying positive things about yourself. You are smart, you are strong, you are caring, you are kind. Do not mention any of your negative attributes. For every negative thing you say, add another minute to the time you spend looking in the mirror. It is your responsibility to build yourself up, no one else's. You can do it. As the days go on, you will find you are having to add less time onto your ten minutes, until finally, you spend just the ten minutes saying completely positive things about yourself. Eventually you will begin to believe them. You are essentially retraining your brain to say nice things to you, rather than mean things.

This society is so bleak, and there are so many mean people who say hateful things while hiding behind a computer screen, and this has cause self esteem rates to go way down.

Build yourself back up to stay above the hatred

Tip Nine- Handle Rejection with Pride

If you have low self esteem, this will be hard, so you have to build yourself up to be able to do this. Otherwise, it will get to you , and make you not want to talk to people any longer. If you are rejected before you build yourself up, just take some time to recuperate.

Not everyone will want to talk to you, especially nowadays. In today's age, people judge others before they even open their mouths, and decide on if a person is “worthy” of speaking to them. You have to break away from this thinking. You also cannot think that someone is above your level, they may seem like they are, and turn out to be the nicest person ever. However, when you approach someone, they may reject you, and this is okay. You may not want to talk to every person that approaches you either.

If you are rejected, shake it off. Remind yourself that it is not you, it is who they are. They decided that they did not want to get to know you, and that is their loss, not yours. Get back up on that metaphorical horse and try again with someone else. You will find someone who is actually worth talking to.

Tip Ten- Don't Latch On

In a setting with a lot of people, it is so easy to try to find one person that you enjoy talking to, and staying with them a majority of the time. This is a bad idea. You have to work the crowd so to speak. How boring would it be if you were at a concert, and the singer only interacted with one fan. It is the same concept with talking to people. Go around to different people, and try to make more than one new friend. Eventually you can come back to that one person, but let them have some time to talk to others, and give yourself time to talk to others as well.

How These Tips Help

These tips are for your own personal use to adapt to specific conversations and situation, and to psych yourself up before you go to a social event where you may not know someone that is there.

Following these tips will give you an edge on your conversations. Using these will help give you a self esteem boost, and you will learn how to help yourself. These tips will make you a better conversationalist and a better you.

Chapter 6

Bonus Tips

If you have tried all of these tips, and find that you still cannot connect with people, you should try to see about getting some help with a psychiatrist. There could be some real deep-seated issues there. Talking to people is hard, but if you have tried to break out of your shell, and find yourself having panic attacks every time, you need to find out what is going wrong.

There is nothing wrong with getting help either. Just as you would need to see a doctor for a physical illness, you should see a psychiatrist if your social anxiety is so bad that it is causing you to break down at the thought of talking to someone you do not know. There are a lot of resources that are at your disposal. If you do not know a psychiatrist in your area, try talking to your normal doctor, and he can help refer you to someone. The best thing about that, is he is more likely to know a specialist to ensure that you are getting the best level of help that you can get.

How to know if it is more than just being shy

- You have panic attacks regularly in social situations: This can be the sign of a serious problem. You should get it checked out, and maybe the doctor can help you figure out how to work through it in a way that is best suited to you.
- You avoid stores during busy hours: If you would rather go without a necessity for a period of time because you do not want to visit a store during busy hours as there will be too many people there, and could cause you to have a meltdown, you should see a

doctor. This is serious. You cannot deny your needs. A doctor can help you figure out the root of the problem, and set you on your way to healing.

- If you feel physically ill in social situations where there are only a handful of people: If being in small groups makes you feel physically ill, you should definitely look into it. Doing so allows you to truly live your life to the fullest, once you figure out what is wrong.

Don't let anxiety control your life any longer. Get the help you deserve, and do not feel bad for doing so. You deserve to live a happy life unrestrained by anxiety. Regain control of your life.

Conclusion

Thank you again for deciding to purchase this book. If you have trouble talking to people, follow the tips you have read, and exercise them in your everyday life. If you have issues with holding a conversation, I hope this book helps you become better at it, and good luck with your endeavors on becoming a better conversationalist.

CPSIA information can be obtained
at www.ICGtesting.com
Printed in the USA
LVHW051711181020
669109LV00035B/1472